there was this bird there was this bird there was this bird there was this bird there was this bird there was this bird there was this bird there was this bird there was this bird there was this bird there was this bird there was this bird

ALSO BY NIKIA CHANEY

To Stir &

us mouth

MEMOIR

Ladybug

FICTION

Three Walking

there was this bird

nikia
chaney

—

poems

POETRY
NORTHWEST
EDITIONS

Everett • Seattle
Washington

Copyright © 2025 by Nikia Chaney

All rights reserved
Printed in the United States of America
First Edition

Cover design by Rachel Kelli
Book design by Abi Pollokoff

Poetry NW Editions is an independent, non-profit educational press in residence at Everett Community College.

Library of Congress Control Number: 2024952889
Names: Chaney, Nikia, author
Title: There was this bird / Nikia Chaney
Description: First Edition / Everett, Washington: Poetry NW Editions, 2025
ISBN-13: 978-1-949166-10-1

Poetry NW Editions
2000 Tower Street
Everett, Washington 98201

www.poetrynw.org

contents

part 1 *scripts*   1

part 2 *love stories*   15

part 3 *the small screen*   25

part 4 *the argument*   37

part 5 *there was this bird*   51

acknowledgments   71

*in this seat you are tall legs like pistons pillars high spines as long as the
orange strips of light a sun rising slick then the
      foam that disappears while here in this
          seat you stumble only slight the
                mouth of rattan woven and bricked around the lips made
or else drawn into paper ribs that can't
   be silent that can't
       not know how to persist
  here where the cloud touches to
taste each eyelash drifting through to
     be here by the side of it the
  audience obedient the
     window framed over with wooden posts that maybe here
          splintered you are soaring you are
               writing a one'd thang
                   you are stuffing every
                      word down and
              starting over
               you are larger than
                    your small you your small
         part here where you start telling a story
             go where more references
are not needed where nothing should be
          easy because the
             kaleidoscope's voices
      all here just be trying
      their best to merge and
          sing the
   correct version into real*

          part 1
         scripts

            now us as
       objective musings a
           theory or two poised

    bar fishing past piss

test strips
    poised bruised pent
        over humans that hover tooled

and unable even in this

musing this covering up of the
              true crime tv the locked
        cage to croon to watch what we say as this

          thought may just be typical this

          cheatsheet humanity's
     bid to leggo the
          soul for this

    theory about escaping prison by watching a screen is

just as thick and serving as fantasy about
            us othered
        men called boys and unwomen or that thing on tv

    seeking of its nonself to

brighten a new name a rightly being that becomes the
    the technique
        of another reduction watching itself boxed

        up skinning into industries like

            horror doled out
     dull aren't these dank
               pieces of life these

           good places to
                    hole up and enter so much
           chatter indigent

everywhere in each cell like bruises at the

                      hub recording
our theorizing waxing us
        here the shuffle of it a kind of

    survival where we can pretend we

comprehend you see
        us as animals you
       portray

       us as dolls you
               dress and we drill
out of the body blackness retrofit in all

     our separate ways

     in what feels like limbo nooks
maybe bound
         postures eyes like flashlights

critical pervasive

        but still lost cause wait a
            minute my
        show is on—streamed

                                            get by

this is the first line: we prefer to say get by, us angels
                                 us moderns squinting in the sun's dark
                            skin gyrating messages that burn

this is a pause here: like something etched in metal or sand
and another pause: like patience
                            a long skirt kissing our thighs lipstick maroon and tender
now a line break:

                            for *just to get by* we say and the emotion rotates
                       to commercial our best selves chattering bells
                         bloating down hallways the
                              rowdy verses flashed into what a forehead could make
or rather a piece
of song: we sing *this morning,* I woke up
                               armpits streaking in the plastered light of
name it this: *get by*
                          like might and want is solved by
                                so many body sounds

and finish the thought
or at least move this up: into what a forehead could make
                               that could burn us all over again
                               we'd say it and mean it
                               we'd hope it we
give an image   swaddled it in our laps with bricklike bags
that will also burn   scarring the arm but all that's left to soothe
seethe and silence   that worry of what bright nail next

this telling paper:
                how we got out just in time
to end: our curved hungry halves half intact but still dancing

or make it the first line and   praying it to just
name it again: *get by, get by*

This show is
My shit. Look
for small places to
Sniff lines. Like
A soap
Opera but
unclean. Tune
It up. Here
She come
curling
Across the
dials. Not
Like this
I say but
I mean like
This. Good. Show
sit.
Unrendered in
Stroke
Every week. Watch
her flailing.
The descent
in ribs or the arms
static
Ready to watch
Wide eyed taped
and seen. Show
How we must
have walked all hunched
Over. The right
to better to

See the strings and
that spree
Hammering its
dark station
break. The stria
Stroking the wire. Saying This struggle
Is you. My show
my girl
on edge Streaming
Is it. The very next fad her machete molded Elbows the
The new
Black my
shit not to
Miss.

You are going to
put
                a frame   /   a piano

in front of a body that   tells that body that this is
the world a pathway gleaming like smog   reaching outwards to ask what that

   tiny body sees
        of
            herself   /   of that which
              as it   is reflected
                 a   personhood build like stacked wood
       wall plastered over.

                You are going to
                    paste   /   stamp
              a sign on the   forehead
                   dank   brush
          belonging in the feen circled
back to become the view scribbled over with gold handprints grasping

       for purchase hairfuls of fists that
                  bear witness

      in the palm   /   in vein
            the anxiety passed down
    in the speaking   howls
        where
                      she   /   we

                needed more

You are going to close eyes

        (you'd better)   /   take the square and carve it
        round set it /   out to dry daylight like
                a button pushed
      by a limb pressing
                      sounds / images
             thoughts into being
                for that little girl is   looking at
     you   waiting
          to see
   herself   it
     unground down

The flowers are barking in this offering of self. The fragrant bloom in bottle. The stem a throat. The weeping this time a portrait groaning in its quaver of colors yellow red exercises that chant the limbs of green into being. Now a wink of glass prism light heavy pickled in cones. Now the pet name of window. Now the posy thunder. The hollow spaces brightening slowly as silent longing fills up. You keep waking to remember. A hum on the edge of bed. You think you can hear it. Clinking. Water. Applause. The smell of skin in tinge sound. You think you asked for impressions. Offerings. Give me savor, you must have said. Print out this toll and entrust its loud voice here. Tell our story again and again in vase framed on counter in kitchen in do rag in bed covers by the window. Like we home.

The flower. Say rebar. King. In this offer of self. The fragment doom. In both let them. Say throated hew heeling time. A portrait groped in a quaver of colors a yell of a red exercise. That chants of limbs green. That being a wink of glass prism lightning heaving lead. Now comes the pet. The name, the window won. The posy thunder, hollows and paces bright and slow. Say silence. Longing filling up. You keep waking. Wanting to remember. Humor this edge of bed. You think you can hear it clinking water. A plausible smell. Say skin. Say tingle. Say sound. You. Thin asked. For this offering gives savior. Say you must have. Say print this out. Toll and entrust the loud voice of our story here again. And again frame the vase. Count the kitchen. Do this rag in bed. Covering the window lies here home.

by whose metric should
you live *by the water* where you should ask

sleeping this thin strands of world beneath
by whose visceral rules *this boneframe of self* this

upending of direction *settling* rightness *weightless* stern

definition and all that is wrong *up* with
this world *outside this container* that

fingertap *of coming*
punishment for both body

and commune *the the places unmade* with what

guidebook does
the personhood *with what good food* needing

resting each frame of us into a complex
learn to whimper *it is waiting* pule or

wander *all that fullness* when you *satisfaction* only seek

to ask *all that abounds*
take to succor *in the slow drip of solidness* from the empty

that is wailing *singing* scratching
fingers on the stomach lining making

red and hollow folds *to the arrival finally met* to

when will this signaling

of others when *when we realize our hands* end us

the we who can connect *touch and breath*

stretch us like soup into the river *slide* the answers

for our questions *out* of our *mouths* myths that are *real*

you paint a
single square that I
watch unmoving the body

love stories spinning the
border in   *the blue knobs*
                                   ribbons of my
         questions melting

                                   making a
                                         kind of narrative of

     laugh tracks and the square
   pack of
                                 grass brittle
                   brown under the green of zipped
fence the house
    fattened with
                  long happy lies
                         its stony
    stamps its clay
feet tv jewels and
          I love   **part 2**
       you like this false and sweet   **love stories**
   earth and hugged fantasy

for our people. I have no people. coconut
oil in pearl
jars. beads that long to dangle on ends of braids. shoes, knotted sandals
that perch patient at the door. I have no door. saying you are here daughter.
I am no daughter. my black skin is too pocked. ragged. each scar
a capital letter of my last name. while stretching before us this has to have
been.
here child. these
inhabitants of heaven. I have no gentle world. open their bellies to you. I
have no
pride. Flowers like ribbons that cut
through each brick. cake. smooth black skin gleaming. I have no insides. I
have scars.
limbs as broken
baskets dangling from tall trees. tongues that want. we want you to
stop trying. I have no sky. your limbs
are still kind. that cup
of being kissed. that slow want. I have no
pathway to reach you ancestor. mother. dear friend. on this desk a cup half
filled.
I have no flower
to place within its open mouth. we gift you
two thin strands of lemongrass. we hide for you honey. we warm the bowl.
use your
own water, fold
your body's old pain into a spoon. I must be this spoon. you are
able to gather what you need. I am no sun. You just shine
and mirror the world.

when you sit down to.
write it down to.
bless it for.

unrequited is.
only yet for.
him or her looking.

this is when.
begging water to.
crawl on.
tongue and skin and.

bodies then.
alone all up in.

I am because.
when you turn to.
this is wanting when.

I still.
blessing only and.

I want to tell you a story where you will stencil on the fall board your gold
a round map that delivers you from the body to mine to the stroll of my
coins an embossment
gridded
vision, the pen held between each of us like the light refracted in each eye, I
want to watch
tv but adapt draw long black lines through the
screen like my arm is rated for you alone
unexpected an apple or laugh track now with a
knob blinking pages into existence where
you may even fall asleep listening imagining that this kind of moving
text burns the back of the
head pinches our corneas raises our palates thousands of feet
from the ground to say this space between us this writer and
reader this producer this watcher this lover and loved are face
scarred
into muscle long ago stretched flat and
mean but so supple we can't keep our
mouths static

                 I want to watch   the movie
         I want to watch   a dragonfly woman's body curved readying
             to lick the scene nfly woman's body curving in front ying
        to lick the scene   an ocean dark boats a flow of face face
         with eye and stroke each boats a flow of face small body like I am
with eye and stroke each   one finger stretched to sun look lit at them
                color look and breathe stretched to sun look feeling a little bit of
 color look and breathe this wandering air eating it small wings it of
                     the view to touch ir eating it small proximity r
         the view to touch it speaks looking back at me
                 this light flowing ng back at me into indexes and codes
         this light flowing   or our blended skines and codes
                   this green blended skin   moment of a first time new
          this green   grass this picture of tree this first time new
                refracted mirror icture of tr slow waiting watching our own
           refracted mirror snaked through ng watching our own
                 snaked through   icons of us between
                          icons of us between

I want to call her a she   but knowing how the old
spittle is not dry yet and   how her
gowns don't gode female   (these old

boys clubs still relocking   doors) I resist and I'd call her
underserved but that   nonbinary sticky

rib   still   gives because   that diva is more
than hormone than raw emote   human
secretion fat culture spilling   from the orifice does

more with words than spit   and maybe she's

Muslim quiet like hijabi   praying all by herself
in academia the thin hall
ways more doors or she   could be split apart

so that names don't attach   spilling instead back
into images of more story   but there are

feathers there ain't it? thick ribs   serrated body
face this body these bodies scraped.   down into

a gathering of work so   perched high in dusty law
books that   the strings of   mornings quivers prostrate
as to how   it all went   down don't   you

see how much   bottom this well goes how

the hope at   the   end of this
well goes to town tasking itself to taste the wires dancing
in the wet air black bodies

Asian, Indigenous, homeless, mentally ill all
knowing their own names

all knowing as they have always been what
they want to have and to be only now miles of   gold robes

caressing their backs like   the wet mouth   is licking clean
the stretched limb readying

it for the scrubbing back of clouds for the crossing

not to run or hide to   but to be read
as a body of work   to be seen
as necessary

            and the bird and the hair and the wave and a bush that hides
        a shaky tail in the iron pleated hand signs and the way it intertwines
              itself into the middle of prayers and
    the fat flesh a closed eye the open need fuzzing and trembling like we (now
the speakers) really could put the maiden all wide-eyed on the beast's chest like
we do do that
whitewash the boil of myth and strain
    innocence of all its bile and
the music dripping its violins one snare to pepper the muscle in rib and that
maltreated hero yenning
  for mercy with
    quietlike spans that cliff us (now the audience) with a new taste of outlook:
        tell me a story complex yet means
            flight means green mossed images means
                insects means bone water in pounding this
              ever present wall means it all the muscle
                ribs walking in tune the human of us melting the
                    birds aflock
                      the stone pathways or rules making us (now
                    anyone) intertwine

part 3
the small screen

like little balls
of wax, their names, quick glimpses
of lives past the borders of the computer screen. how you know
to line them

up by letter by time spent by headrest by itching toes. how you know to walk, write,
popping speak, brazen like that twisting fire impressions
of your tales on soft foreheads reedy chips that punch loud as vessel
sounds

and where you go, what's that dark thing you keep pressing, the one that curves back
on the beginning in a slighted lie to illustrate the scripture
of the what was found

yesterday, the chafe as gold as the ash, the heed at the end,
rearing its backside to hog undocked and tepid prayers into its sternum

completelike and ever
unseen. you tend to want more. you tend to
interpret, grade, you complain about repetitions. but
maybe the yolk of a thing the
candlelight ain't meant for campsite. maybe

it is there in the marbles hard or soft mixed up in bowl. sorted out. it
felt good didn't it. it
made it to stage, dolled up, threads gleaming.

and hey you left it here for me to find.

There are seven versions to this story, one is here,

the second is in the brown of his eyes, what he would see if I stood by the shoulder a pathway petaled and curling around the ankle, a man that broke my arm

the third is the way our child squints like him face folded in smooth lines

the fourth is just words black pressed on white lost in the back of a book, violence those words say, love those words read, time

I say I'm going to rub my stomach then her feet, I say I'm taking my daughter to the beach. I say I'm going to go down to the water and float like a whale beached and bleating in that cold half water half sand and remember to forget. I'm going to drink milk, the whole carton, with this child, reconcile this untenable thing then squat and unpick fat locks until the seven versions interpolate themselves into a now a space that finally feels good.

the fifth is the cut of the sand wet and sordid, there a string of trailing again in the dirt, like the way I lose the thought of it all when this child reaches out for me dances with me in the cleaning, her small hums my howl my entire being the fire setting itself to eat away at the vessels still broken like curves and waves,

the sixth a name with four letters then when the words hit the end of the mouth the note shifts and raises a skirt to scream to the world,

we who live = well we = who speak we = who vote we
at top we = who see we who = press we who = rot we
who are we the = people we the = peace = thriving to
try = we that weep un = connected to = bends of holy
ness in = to imps and = fiends we = who went = dined
on the win = d we who wind = dirt and wa = ter who =
in the a = bility to make the = selves blind to a = not
her cruel story = accept = ratings = marks and proper
= ty lines = territ = ories with s = kin where the = tone
of it al= so binds the push = unnecessarily the = med
icine = a fabric of ho = we who a = re we who a = re w
ho = we are who we say we = are part = ici = pant = a
cons = tit = uent citi = zen prost = itute per = sonhoo
d en = tity un = hum = aned be = ing drawn in pix =
els spl = ayed out bo = dies = all bra = ss te = chnical

what to
do with
the it of
it the diagrams the
blue chubbed
snippets of
conversations all
shiny in
their insistence to
be the
heard
letters lying
prone beneath the
hard bright
lines like narrative is
just
nostrils space open
joyous as as
riding in
flaunting cups
of coffee holding
tenderness and
what of the
whipcadence then the
word smart
play sewn in
ink and
spit on

                    card   white
              breadpaper   where
                 teased crisp you
                    you said
         us   would tell
               later about   how
             well we   were
                 actually and
             how
                 doing
                      n
                eat i much of
              g   song this is
                       and

                 plopping the   f
             fortune of ownedness   o
                                     r
              into pools of   m
                                     u
                     methods   l
                to chord   a
                                     s
                as if even   the
         law
             were   as
                  zipper   th i
                                 n
               as the
         unwined vinegar curved
                 on a   l
                            istening
             head
                 to tel
                    me how to
                 wr
                  ite it so
                     you judge
                  you

audience tell
          me what to
    do now with
this   and   stories
          these
              written
                 embodied doodads
newly   shiny
       flapping
    like they   thighs
was all shimmied

         on neon feathers
    tickling
         closed
             fold
  each
              say dreams
            of
              scream
       scene cut seen
               we
            baby
       back blinding stage
                              honey
  center we tilting
             you

                we   can
    others free   each
         finally breaking
  all   in perform
     lost

and wanting
us to see she refutes
a little
bit of everything: the way
others' eyes stay closed,
the capital L of labor, mother
hood in only women
hood black,
the door
sound slamming its
finality into sprays
of thin dust in every room the image
of herself
not herself *no* she
says that
if this were
correct then
it would want the pickings
apart of its gooey laces
the transformations
of representation
in body becoming
like two people learning
how touch changes
the skin how gaze
wanders back
to enjoy
the view I am only
correct when I
dance with
your slight wrongness

let it
agitate us both into
something purple and *yes* she
says smiling
for it would have to smile in
refutation
all these new
ways laying the thick
of the argument
into tangible interwoven
plays both
sides now
multiplex as if those
feelings of being
seen were really all we
could
be sure of as you
said that mornin
into my ear full of conviction
let me differ let me
use
your mouth's sound
breath thought-tongue as my
own paint me
patchwork make me
contemporary the frame
of all our fingers
new
things
here bloom

I will put myself in the glass walls and wait for an unknown arm to grasp the neck and throw me. My rabbit ears twitching. My cat tail tucked. I will watch the sand spin green tan below magnified grains big as crab rocks sweat prints begging to filled with the salt water hardness and heat of foam and swell. I am small. But not so small this bottle does not squeeze the fur. The heat of this. The thrill of soar. When I hit the water for now the bottle has decided to speak I coo. No I purr. Then I twitch. How not to get wet. How to find in broken shards only friend lover self. How to change self from one creature to something not yet made. One with curved thick bottomed glass. One with skin too brown to win. I am not rabbit. I am not bottle. But I want to be. I want to be a piece of paper that someone takes to give away. I want to be a bit of softness that codes friendly. Then me and that bottle and that dank hole and those big feet can hurry. Our whiskers touching each blade of grass as we run away. As if being found and stroked and read and run is the same as fences falling away. As if there really are monsters hairy sea shapes climbing out of their buzz beasts that can catch me dig us both out and sprinkle our pulp on new shores.

        what hole
    did it
agonize out of to
   twist that
      scratching fullness in
my ear like a
          bite from a clipped
      insect insisting
         on crip-walking through
     my sheets this
       woke object this
   sentient kink of
tool purposed
        waxed
        and mindful for
          I didn't
    ask it to needle
     me ask it
    to unravel the process
      of want from my
  head matter make the
       threads of the unconscious
         actualities that
     vibrate clear flat
meaning and I might not
    have even minded
      yawning slowly up
  if the bite drew
       blood to mix
    with its soft spit

the pillow becoming
            a petri
dish a flowering
                pan a newspaper
        crinkled impossibly
    soaked in stain that I
getting up getting
            down can
almost read

you sit me down to horror to tell me tales the dark
    night stumbling in stranger a lonely metronome

    of failing water like claim and hold your
    voice a tension so slow I am meant to peer

    through the sliver of stain the heavy word where the arguments
    create visions of us as unwhole wieldy holding the

    weapons point blast on each other all us monsters slap
    cratching bold slips of the throat to blame and spit out fear

    but I tend to listen slant then disbelieve argue back
    your granite logic pretend liquid your hard shoes pressing wet

    prints on my forehead for inside this thin brow
    is a tenderness that cold boils an agency saying

    hell no I disrespect peering over the edge of the glass
        begging to make you over and listen to **part 4, *the argument***

I imagine that the shackles are for intimacy. To touch the skin of the ankle, to caress and caress until the keloid sighs and breathes in the smell of dust, uncut hay or swamp. I picture the chain as the hug, winding its pillow metal around the waist holding the body back from the brink. Love. Falling. Intimacy doubled into self. Knife sticking out the back to curve and pierce the heart again. Fists that stop to kiss before they dance. I imagine my palms were large enough to place the body on a pedestal, hands and feet splayed, more chains of want and spin. The flapping sound. The numbers going down. The hope that it will stop. I make the body your body then mine. I say push. I say it does not hurt. Then it's a thousand years later. In my hand a microscope. A spur from an old would. The hint of a mark just barely raised. There is a voice like a witness peering from above. A dirty dish. An answer for why that makes sense. I imagine that these were and weren't lies. I imagine that I imagine. Then triple it multiply it ask to go back in time anything to not sit here bounded to the bounded to.

       Your humanness
          represented in penis and muscle the breath of you
        testosterone height and baritone your eye
      blind to small things you
    christian european you religion first then
when you hint at the real aim your skin you friend who
makes an other
scrawl x to punctuate a bondage
between us all and your ribs heaving creating two worlds
 of mind impressing a kind
  of reality on the othered a raw
    fantasy where you sit at the center throan your aloneness
     and your opaqueness your world swimming forever in a
      psychotic sea

If you could climb would you become of them what you see the pain of what you have done
If you went down could you bear

        Your humanness hidden unmoored unseen
          though your body gives out life
            and your strength is in knowing
              intimately all the names of pain
                and what is above
                  at the end of open legs
                  the land slowly ceded
              in the gathering the pressure of one more day you
             of them you of bottom you of sign your name
              in the play of this game where winning
              costs even ever more the truth a heavy
                stoney in the belly
                 of your scattered
              body flating always prone

for bell hooks

The world is a thin skinned man sitting by a lake. He tosses in a pebble to make the water ripple. Birds startle and fly black against the empty sky. The man looks down and makes up names for what he sees.

   The world is the bird perched by the lake. The bird watches the man and waits.
       The movement of a tiny pebble gives the bird its feathered skin. It moves
            all its wings back to push air and gravity and cloud and mist to
      make its many bodies sing.

                The world is a pebble damp then dry then wet. The pebble
                          blinks
                  and turns its
                                cold skin to the bottom of the
                                      lake
              where it settles to make
                        itself a new home. It
                        digs in laughing.
                                          It preens.

The world
is a lake.

     Its water cupped in its hands. Its song the slant
of light the flying birds the caked dirt bed of rock large and small the landing
          of air tasting its flowing skin. The lake names itself lake names the
                world lake

becomes a small part of every
        whole and unhungry thing.

The world is ignorant on purpose. The world breaks the water loses the pebble pushes away the bird takes the man and drapes his pale skin over every eye it can.

        The world is a brown woman writing theories about love. She is
                following the ping of the rock into an
            establishing the black birds into a fearless dance
              of group the burble of the water flat and
                wide under her own skin. She
      notes the negative image of the man. She notes
                  how he does not
                see. She understands now the
        now of this
        tingling feathering
              feeling it feeling herself
                unnaming
                  and remaking
              the flat edges of the
            world.

after Cheryl I Harris

I chattel and see linked arms the iron pressed to ankle the way work swells in the mouth to press back to memories of more than being owned

II time here too
much no time no
space too break
time work seconds
to centuries to more
time to too much
not enough no
break time wait
and make time bend
back time too hard
too lose

III home be looking up at the bottom
of the pan from the floor

the undersides black and burned in flakes
and the taste of iron where rest

and sleep don't work this hard
where space is made to fill

IV nobody's land occupied stolen took sold dirt suck out of hand theft broke took nothing and you got nothing and you can't leave this place and you can't win

V your body heavy like
a pregnant belly but
light-like and on
the toes don't
you remember
joy or soaring some
where all that
cloud and light look
down at
the crown of heads
the tiny
figures bending
over the fields as
wide as palms here
they look so far away
but down there up
close they press
themselves so close
to you you
shake

VI before there were owners before there were crowns before
the repose before the zombies before ideas of man as beast
before the beast is bad before the social line before the
contracts before the sound of horns before the cities state before the legs
went bad before the hunger before the break before the break before the
break before the wrong

VII once there was a
break in the how
we did things

        we stayed home and
left work we looked

    at the edges
        of the broken systems
              that turn our
lives quiet alone into
    a waiting
space asking
    always to breathe

VIII here is a line you
go there you I go
here and you sit
down and wait

IX every story is the same: you trying to erase what I am

X this is a debt that must be
repaid cause its settled with skin

XI Am I
really
owned
by you?

XII sometimes an eye closes
shuts down its lid to
sink back into the couch
the wide green sea

as calm and false
as the way the line between

us stretches longwise
pushing the body back

making the divide impossible
to bridge our arms now
by our sides

XIII say something anything
else
change this
thing
look up from
it
try
finally
a different story

shall I then rage again. this meat as only view here rushing into dice and rocks trying to open the bile to turn the bitter liquid back to steam. turn and it gyrates into the same damn mirror. curse and it is still you. you and the cave. you and the cellophane. square-piped and sandwiched between my sunrise born but failed questions. pillow trafficked on impossible rivers like curdles that lose knives or breadcrumbs to the floor. sharp as bones. shall I then call you. piss into the worms schmoozing eyelids. reach into the backseat. say come here and let me control the way you express your love to me. you are too pale. too paranormal. impossibly pegged. ready to dive back each fool verse 'bout how I wandered into the warehouse with my lips smacking. udders all full begging for this crypt. the loneliness a pipe of flesh hollowed out. my marrow was never enough to drink the sale of it. a bit of history terraformed in flesh. do you dare ask what I think what I'd actually do if I had the throat permission to sate this hunger. aren't you scared. aren't you burnt enough.

~~don't make heaven so~~
~~dark child so full~~
~~of voices and arguments and~~
~~stick like bashing~~
~~sounds that portend their own~~
~~kind of irrepressible~~
~~theory you forget to~~
~~beg to read so bruised~~
~~little girl so injured that~~
~~the pores white~~
~~boards flexing their~~
~~smooth noses down at~~
~~each head to trim~~
~~dimness true blemish~~
~~sun blot duct and thonged~~
~~old affronts contuse~~
~~anxious blind ways old~~
~~black out curtains to~~
~~make solution history a~~
~~black box an~~
~~anodyne grumbling and~~
~~spitting forth answers into~~
~~its own body and you can't~~
~~see how it works so~~
~~you imagine dusty~~
~~black holed square~~
~~jaws that itch to trap a~~
~~thin limb so dark~~
~~girl why does it have~~
~~to be so sullen so~~
~~flat and devoid of pearl~~

cogs ~~instead many striated~~
slivers of ~~soft button the~~
machine now ~~a~~
rainbow now ~~a cloud now the~~
sound ~~tipping~~
ask~~ing permission to write you~~
~~small glinting your own~~
~~gold at the~~ kneel

there was this bird once there was this **part 5 *there was this bird*** *once there was this*

A combination of voices, laughter, sound: people like so many knives and forks and music. We smile drunk, high. All we can hear are waves We run our hands over the fabric, we feel the music and the fabric. Our body

sharp in the drawer. There is a smear our hand. The couch is plush and soft as sand. that demands we find our balance. Yes we grin. There is a couch a head hovering before us. This head is sound. This head is attached to a white sweatshirt, a new head together with another head. Both heads are moving back and forth to the beat of the music. We watch and feel warm. We pause, fascinated, and we are a third head, unseen, unnoticed. We so want to stare some more but the room changes is smooth pliable, our breath short like touching ourself under cold water

We are watching ants on the sidewalk. We are loving the way they scurry around the red popsicle drip. We love the way the ants walk in straight lines, their zigzaggy lope, their intense speed in black purpose. Us, bent over watching ants and our knee is pressed to the sidewalk. If there were grass here or real yards like the pictures of the cartoon house in the first grade class, we would have been clutching the green blades, digging fingers deep into the green earth. But there is only sidewalk warm from the sun, white light, plain, hard. We are alone here. One ant shape, shifts, and we are in a different moment, a sharp, biting moment, stumbles away heading for freedom, a crack in the sidewalk. We raise our finger and smash it down hard into the ground.

We have been searching through the closet looking for random things we could use. A notebook, a white sock that vaguely matched one in our drawer, old lipstick tube we could dig out with a q tip. Two black sandles, one with a broken strap, a bag full of scarves. A church hat, sent pu s, letters from a man called Kalib. Our mother smiling from a graduation photo, all false lashes and hips. A one-legged barbie doll, shiny blond hair cut down to the scalp. Cords knotted up. A blue leather purse, wigs and more wigs. The pressing comb had been hiding inside the right foot of a black rubber boot. We had registered it, but left it alone, as we spy a pair of jeans that looked like they could fit. We are so excited about the jeans that we leave the pressing comb inside the boot, and push the boot to a far side of the closet. We are happy we did this, otherwise we might never have found the comb again. And there it was, the black boot, pouting in the corner, and inside the treasure the comb. the comb was black, old, with burn marks etched in the wood, a few prongs in the comb bent. We will be beautiful we think smiling.

We
move through
the house, our
body bumping
the door frames, our body
against the furniture,
our finger running
along on the edge of the
couch, an arm brushing a
wall, a foot dragging softly on
the floor. We know this house
the way she knows our face. Each
picture is a memory of balancing on a
chair, or the familiar movement of our hand
brushing away hair to search for a nail. The walls
are colored in time as well: red, last year; brown, ten
years ago; blue, the day I moved in. Waterman and
Mill. So different then. We pause at a mirror on the
wall. Hair gray lines under our eyes, but our eyes
our eyes still the same after all of these years. We
will always be able to recognize ourself by those
eyes. We place two hands on either side of our
face. Our hands are cool, our face is warm. We press
our hands together harder, lifting the elbow up, clenching
what is left of our teeth. We can feel our pulse through our skin.
We can feel our face bones. We squint. Outside Santa Ana winds tear
through the wall, angry ghosts come to take an old lady home. We smile
at that thought. There are things to do in the
kitchen, calls to make. The floor needs
to be redone, the plants
brown and dying
outside. But now
in the mirror we
want this time
to ourselves
. Can we
be?

19 In this room there are maybe twenty women.

The women's heads are turned down, staring at the door in raptly.

We copy the other women.

We like to compare the scarves. Blue with flowers, brown and white stripes,. black with gold

The blue scarf was thrown over the woman's head haphazardly, a little hair peeking out

We were married three weeks ago. This is how to be a proper Muslim. This is how to be a good wife.

We watch each woman in the room, run our eyes over their clothes.

We believe that we are brave enough to ask a question.

Our neck is beginning to ache.

It is easier to concentrate on scarves only.

The   brown   carefully   intricately pinned.

A sheik will speak to us from behind a curtain.

He will answer questions. We wait together. 19

kicking inside our torso. Quick pops that come in

looking. Some stranger   clusters

                    brought us

          pop bubbles

                    and

                              sticky bubblegum. Maybe for lunch a bagel and cream cheese.

Dust swirls in the air, making the sunlight look dirty instead of bright. But dirty or not the sunlight is hot and we feel the sweat

we can't control. Our body is stretched from the breasts to the torso to the hips to pelvis. We think of our ribs a

back to life, pushed the water out of our lungs and we coughed back to life. We think this

watch how the shadow changes in the light. We blink and yawn debating on counting the small ying specks. We can feel the baby

through sluggish grass with a heavy load. Years ago we were yve and we drowned in the ocean when mama wasn't

crying in our arms, happy to see us, awake at last from some underwater dream. Soda

will be the baby coughing

elastic bands and our legs as stalks to wade

from our brow drip down into our eyes. We raise one finger and

We meet a man today. He has a scar that ripples down the left side of his face. He has a wide mouth and dirt that is caked in the roads and lines of his face and skin. He sits on the ground and we think somehow this all must make sense. 20 minutes ago a woman stepped over the man and walked on her way. She had heels on and the sound of the hard soles of the metal made us look up from our book. We look at the man and see he is looking at us and we smile and make up a need that gives us an excuse to ask him something, anything shows our needs. We adjust the pin on our like a creature held down on some scientist's brown board. We see him nod and smile and turn to us and think of all the ways we can talk about being invisible. We imagine telling this man that we feel that he understands. But he slurs his words and turns from us and the light around us shifts from white to coal black to gray.

He moves and we sigh in unison in shadowy space, Our hand is small in the being connected like this strange as if the room is itself a soft piece of rest. too. We soak in his form on the bed.

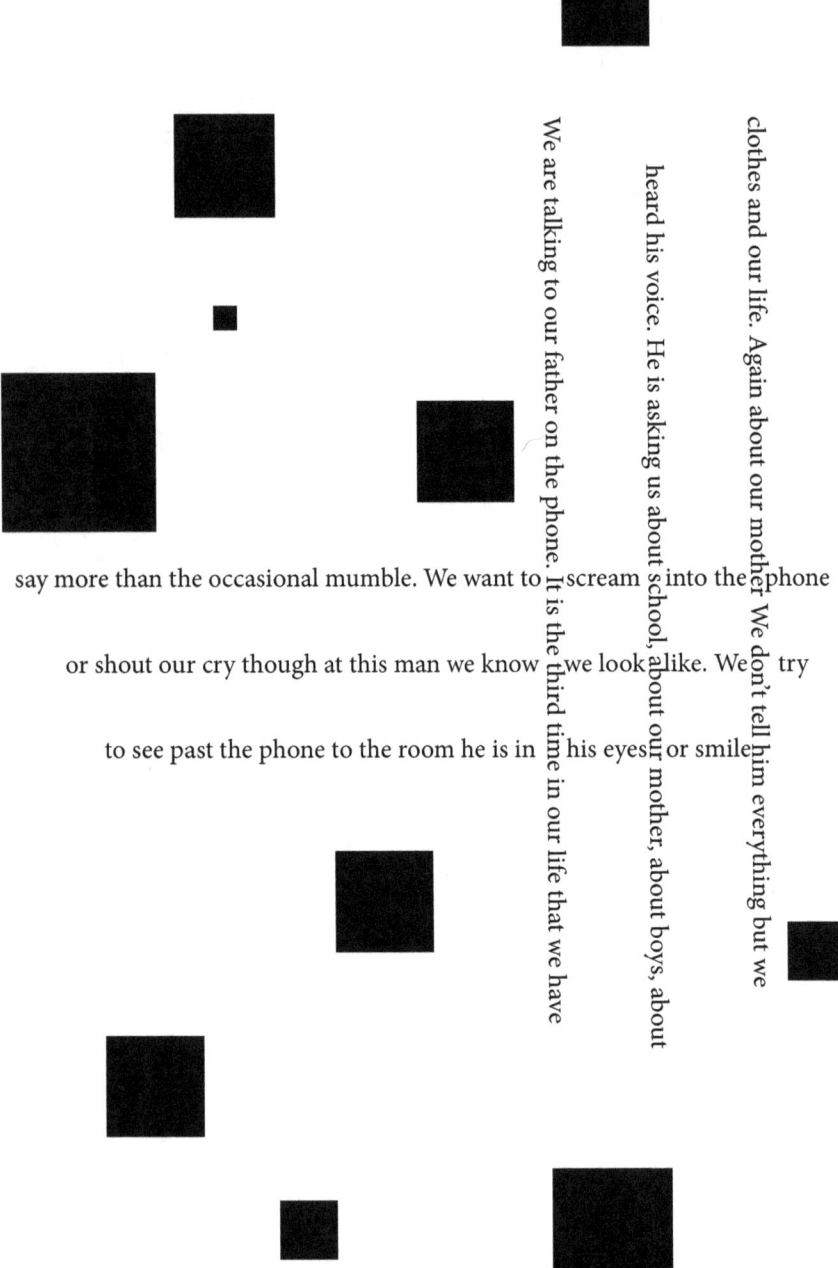

We are talking to our father on the phone. It is the third time in our life that we have heard his voice. He is asking us about school, about our mother, about boys, about clothes and our life. Again about our mother. We don't tell him everything but we say more than the occasional mumble. We want to scream into the phone or shout our cry though at this man we know we look alike. We try to see past the phone to the room he is in his eyes or smile

So instead this first day of teaching we pretend. They are looking at us in symmetrical rows staring at our face expecting us to know what to do. We don't know what to do. Could we really hold this entire class in our hands and soft voice.

We tug on our shirt. There is a tall boy behind us in the line laughing at something someone has said. We do not like the boy and we notice his sound all loudness and hunger and swag and shit and attitude. We tug again on our shirt. We start to count. 8 can sit at a table 3 groups of tables 4 tables + 5 extra chair, and the corner 4 tables outside = 144 seats all together, 3 and one half times more seats outside than inside. 144 = 12 squared so that only the number of girls in Mrs. Henderson's 4th period PE class could sit in a different seat each day. We hope we don't have to prove ourself or move or speak in all this crowd when the tall boy pushes our shoulder on purpose.

trace the sparse hair from ear to chin, the smell of him on our skin, the want their happy orange. We are searching for things to feed ourself. We the wet, on his chest, are in love. A mist of water sprays the green, an Amazonian forest, us warriors with carts. He is kissing our neck. We put our hand in and the soft spray. Even the eggplants looking like so many timne rocks among the bush concur. Heaven is being hungry in a grocery store the hard door slamming our sandled feet. We carefully inspect the vegetables. Such green, such lush green leaves. We don't want to be in a grocery store at 11 p.m., but we are hungry. We feel our skirt swishing through our thighs, reaching with our whole self for a fistful of green.

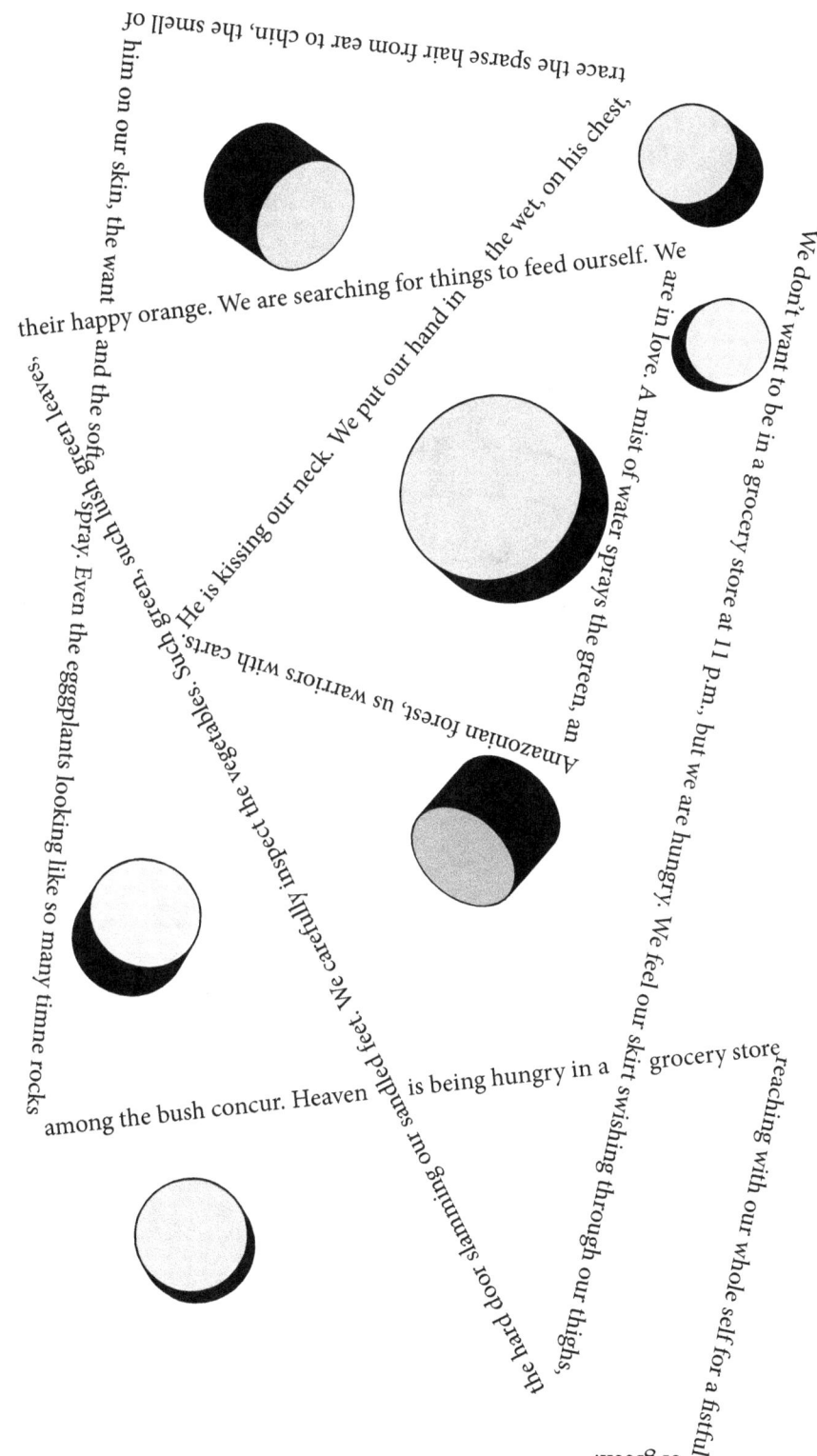

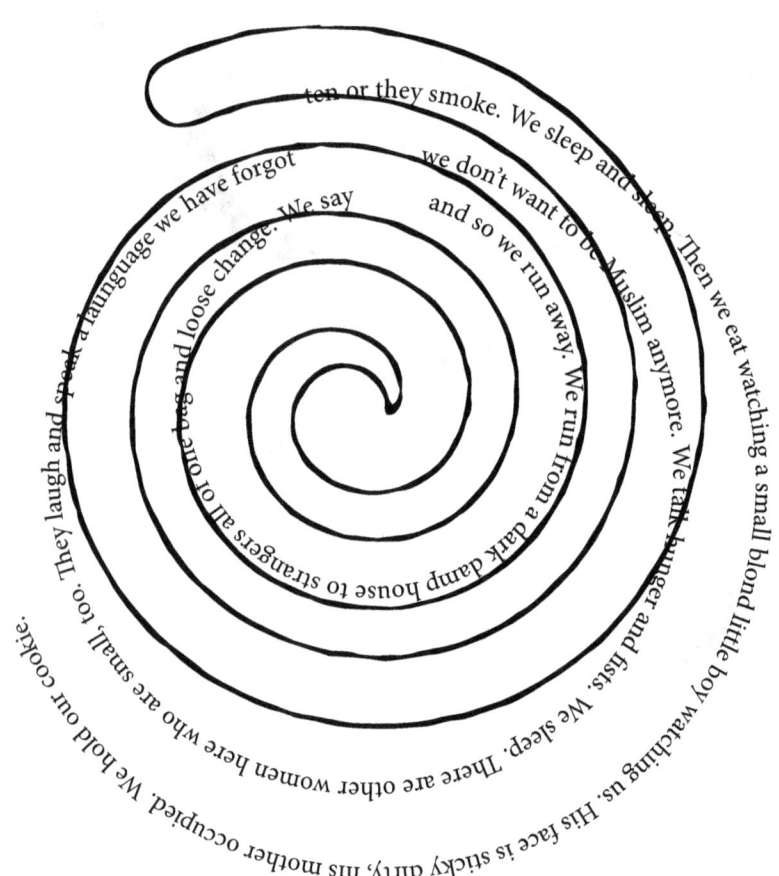

ten or they smoke. We sleep and sleep. Then we eat watching a small blond little boy we don't want to be Muslim anymore. We talk hunger and fists. We sleep. There are other women here who are small, too. They laugh and speak a language we have forgot and so we run away. We run from a dark damp house to strangers all of ours bag and loose change. We say watching us. His face is sticky dirty, his mother occupied. We hold our cookie.

The surgery. Even the word sounds deceptive, like a thing that could if we squinted hard enough be sweet, but underneath sickly and poor. Our back, really our spine and our body empty of food. The room is white and pastel blue. We take our shoes off, then our socks, then our pants. Shirt then bra, then gown. Then their socks, rubber on the soles.

Maybe sickness is the new black. We don't want no damn cure.

Heal me, they say, and we ignore, wait for the rest to be real. Our nurse had a lazy eye. The orderly to be real. Our nurse had a lazy eye. The orderly pushing forward to scream out their own need. the fear to drive us forth.

We think about how our body becomes enemy, how even the cells can revolt.

Take out tissue that is suspect. Then operate on our breasts. We will go unconscious. They will take out strange tools.

Our doctor was balding. His hairline pulling back from the scalp slowly as if it were too afraid

mama

mouth

suck taste touch

handboneskin

when our how in by

warm full

see hear shhape we are

alone

get

up we crawl moveshakesleep

It feels really good to us to have a home
It feels really good to us to have a home

It feels really good to us to have a home

It feels really good to us to have a home
It feels really good to us to have a home

It feels really good to us to have a home

It feels really good to us to have a home
It feels really good to us to have a home
It feels really good to us to have a home

It feels really good to us to have a home
It feels really good to us to have a home

It feels really good to us to have a home

It feels really good to us to have a home
It feels really good to us to have a home
It feels really good to us to have a home

It feels really good to us to have a home

It feels really good to us to have a home

It feels really good to us to have a home

It feels really good to us to have a home

It feels really good to us to have a home
It feels really good to us to have a home
It feels really good to us to have a home

It feels really good to us to have a home

It feels really good to us to have a home
It feels really good to us to have a home
It feels really good to us to have a home
It feels really good to us to have a home
It feels really good to us to have a home
It feels really good to us to have a home
It feels really good to us to have a home
It feels really good to us to have a home

It feels really good to us to have a home

It feels really good to us to have a home

It feels really good to us to have a home

It feels really good to us to have a home

It feels really good to us to have a home

It just be a method be a tool be a place for reckoning as if on purpose the
whitening of the shell as
if the once upon it be grinning to beckon you into a smoke filled tent those
red and gold pillows
like gateways to your own childhood a lap so soft and spread the whole
family of you can fit and
story shifting eyes to bring that almost remembered beat into the hum in
breath like tv like
smoke like bending be its own summer jubilee I'm so howling at y'all right
now story says bird says I'm
gathering you fool bodies into me where the black between each of us
shines out of its own little
eye blinking new worlds all these ages laid out here at all these names for
written over then crossed
out like sound so it can start winding itself into the soft parts of head a
small is in that tale letters of
brown flesh that contain if not muscle then a yolk a sternum yellow joy
stuffed with veins stuffed with
shit memories tendons a way of being a tiny crack appearing something
warm and wet pushing
out settling in these dark rooms waiting to dry words perched hungry on
the beak

acknowledgments

To the incredible team at Poetry Northwest, thank you for your belief in this work and your commitment to amplifying voices that speak to the complexities of our shared humanity. Sound is life and winning this prize means more than you can know. Your guidance and care have made this journey a joy, and I'm deeply grateful for the platform you've given me.

To my family, I love you all so very much. Thank you for being my soul.

To my friends, and my community: Thank you for holding me close.

This work would not exist without all of you. My story would not be with you all.

With so much love,

Nikia

The poems on pages 55–69 were featured in After the Pause *magazine in 2016.*

Nikia Chaney is a multigenre author and visual artist. She has published two poetry books, *To Stir &* (Word Works, 2022) and *us mouth* (University of Hell Press, 2018); a memoir, *Ladybug* (Indlandia, 2022); and a short volume of science fiction, *Three Walking* (Bamboo Dart, 2021). She has serves as Inlandia Literary Laureate (2016–2018). In 2023, she won a California Arts Council Established Artist Individual Fellowship. She teaches in Santa Cruz.

Possession Sound Poetry Series

Sierra Nelson, *The Lachrymose Report*

Lauren Hilger, *Morality Play*

Katharine Whitcomb, *Habitats*

Nikia Chaney, *there was this bird*

Poem text set in Minion Pro OTF with
front and back matter titles in Futura STD.
Book design by Abi Pollokoff
Printed on archival quality paper

Poetry NW Editions is an independent,
non-profit educational press in residence
at Everett Community College.

Founding Editor: Kevin Craft
Managing Editor: Abi Pollokoff

www.ingramcontent.com/pod-product-compliance
Lightning Source LLC
Chambersburg PA
CBHW052122070526
44586CB00016B/2045